Highlights™

창의력 쑥쑥 숨은그림찾기™

Hidden Pictures™

표지 그림 _ 록키 풀러 Rocky Fuller

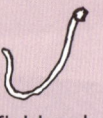

golf club
골프채

fishhook
낚싯바늘

umbrella
우산

artist's brush
그림붓

slice of
cake
케이크 조각

School's Out! 야외수업하는 날

mallet
나무망치

pen
만년필

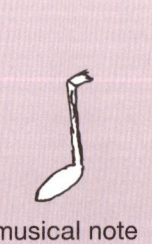

musical note
음표

radish
무

magic wand
마술 지팡이

wristwatch
손목시계

safety pin
안전핀

spoon
숟가락

2

ice-cream
cone
아이스크림 콘

mitten
벙어리장갑

carrot
당근

mushroom
버섯

toothbrush
칫솔

pencil
연필

pushpin
푸시핀(압정)

Illustrated by Charles Jordan

spatula
주걱

wishbone
V자형 뼈

flashlight
손전등

ice-cream bar
막대아이스크림

whale
고래

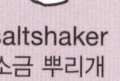

saltshaker
소금 뿌리개

Highlights **3**

Pepperoni, Please 페페로니 주세요

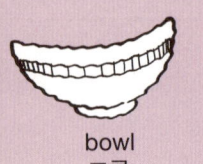

bowl
그릇

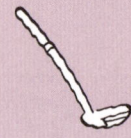

golf club
골프채

feather
깃털

mitten
벙어리장갑

sailboat
돛단배

button
단추

snake
뱀

worm
벌레

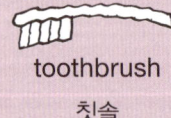

toothbrush
칫솔

party hat
파티 모자

teacup
찻잔

cupcake
컵케이크

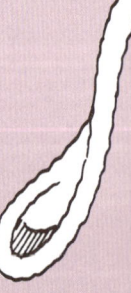

spoon
숟가락

Highlights

Carousel Ride 회전목마 타기

fishing pole 낚싯대
zipper 지퍼
teacup 찻잔
slice of pie 파이 조각
crescent moon 초승달
horseshoe 편자(말발굽에 붙이는 쇳조각)
pear 배
musical note 음표
ring 반지
snake 뱀
screw 나사
golf club 골프채
mug 머그잔
needle 바늘
pennant 삼각기
question mark 물음표
fishhook 낚싯바늘
nail 못
arrow 화살

Hiding the Bone 뼈다귀 숨기기

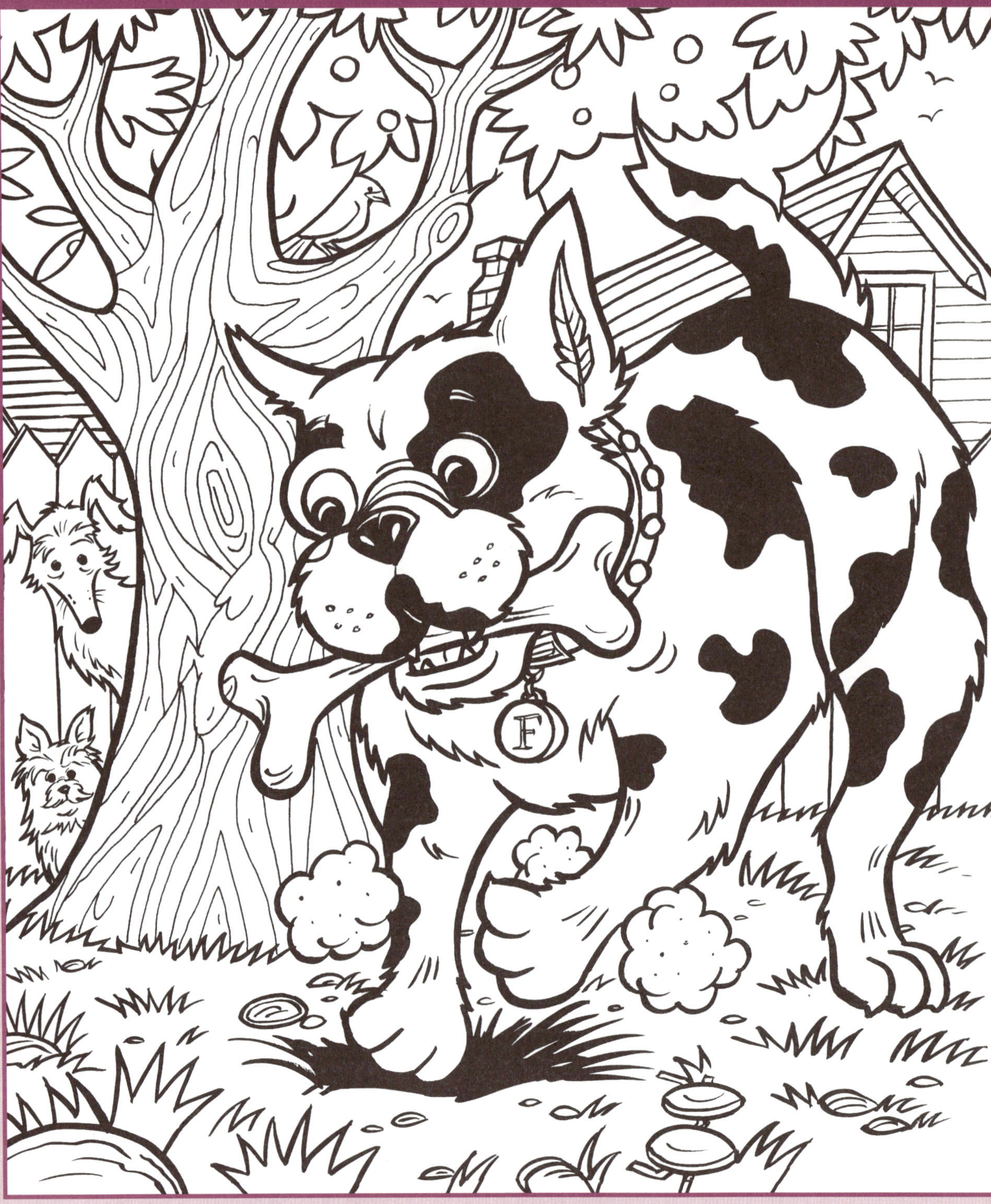

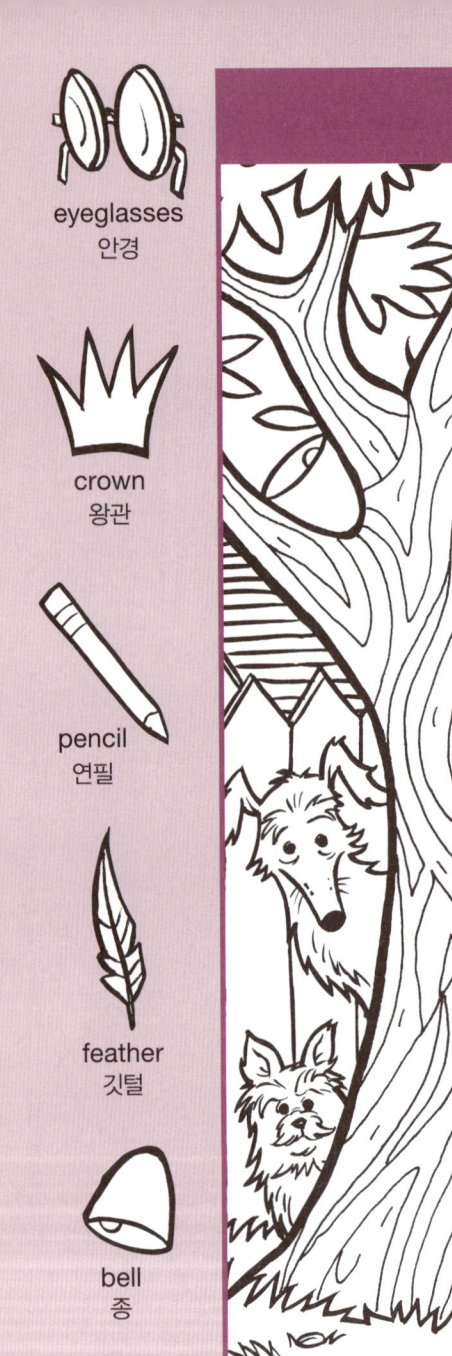

eyeglasses
안경

crown
왕관

pencil
연필

feather
깃털

bell
종

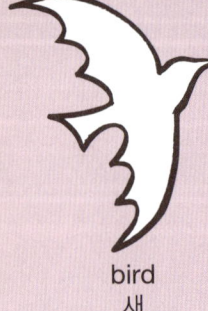

bird
새

glove
장갑

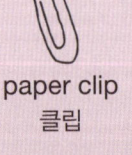

paper clip
클립

ring
반지

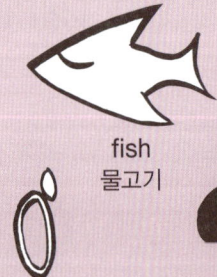

fish
물고기

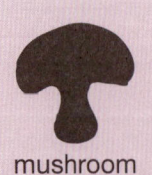

mushroom
버섯

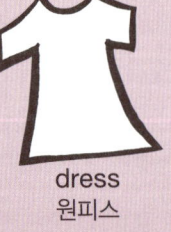

dress
원피스

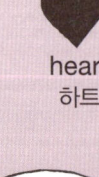

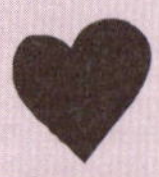

heart
하트

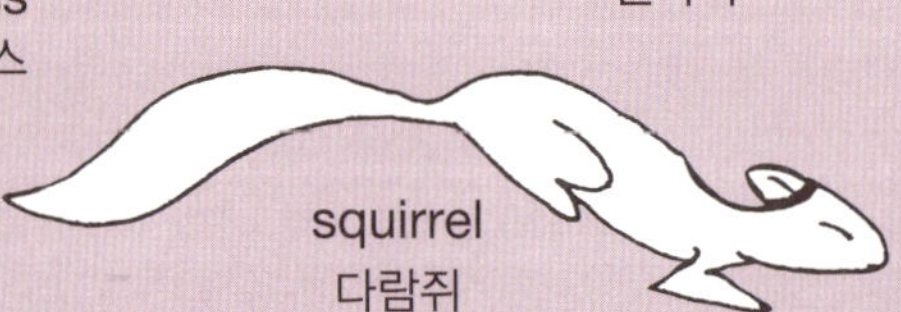

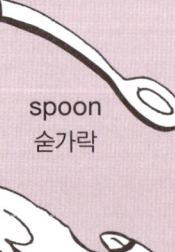

squirrel
다람쥐

spoon
숟가락

ice-cream cone
아이스크림 콘

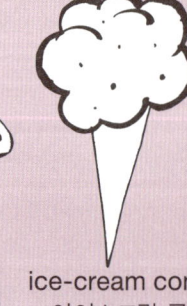

screwdriver
드라이버

safety pin
안전핀

envelope
봉투

iron
다리미

saucepan
냄비

toothbrush
칫솔

wishbone
V자형 뼈

Fishing Trip 즐거운 낚시여행

Illustrated by Leslie Franz

coffeepot
커피포트

television
텔레비전

paintbrush
페인트붓

slice of pie
파이 조각

sock
양말

pencil
연필

carrot
당근

Highlights 7

golf club
골프채

tube of
toothpaste
치약튜브

paintbrush
페인트붓

flag
깃발

crescent
moon
초승달

hatchet
손도끼

teacup
찻잔

toothbrush
칫솔

hat
모자

candle
양초

pencil
연필

slice of cake
케이크 조각

comb
빗

drinking straw
빨대

Illustrated by R. Michael Palan

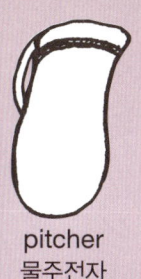
pitcher
물주전자

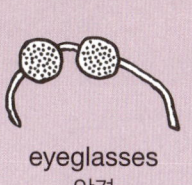
eyeglasses
안경

candle
양초

sailboat
돛단배

canoe
카누

dragonfly
잠자리

City Harvest 도시에서 추수해요

레이크우드
지역주민들의
정원

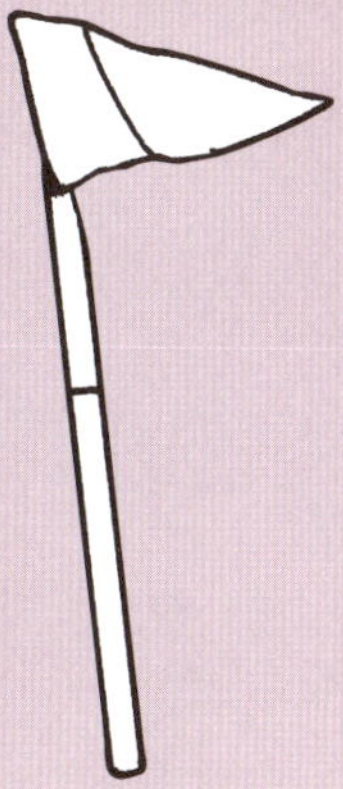

pennant
삼각기

sock
양말

comb
빗

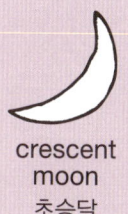
crescent moon
초승달

trowel
꽃삽

ax
손도끼

boot
부츠

Fish School 물고기 학교

ice-cream cone
아이스크림 콘

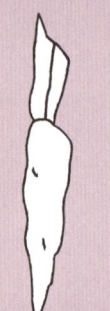

carrot
당근

ruler
자

ring
반지

crown
왕관

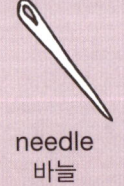

needle
바늘

envelope
봉투

light bulb
백열전구

heart
하트

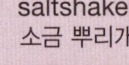

saltshaker
소금 뿌리개

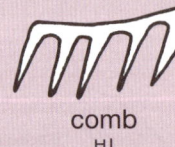

comb
빗

snake
뱀

Highlights

toothbrush
칫솔

heart
하트

ring
반지

mallet
나무망치

butterfly
나비

tack
압정

candle
양초

lizard
도마뱀

mouse
쥐

comb
빗

worm
벌레

safety pin
안전핀

ice-cream cone
아이스크림 콘

baseball bat
야구방망이

saltshaker
소금 뿌리개

needle
바늘

open book
펴놓은 책

crescent moon
초승달

funnel
깔때기

flashlight
손전등

hammer
망치

slice of pizza
피자 조각

Shower Soccer Practice 빗속의 축구 연습

Illustrated by Larry Daste

Lion Gets a Trim 사자의 머리 손질

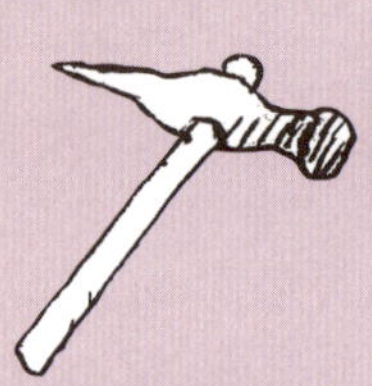

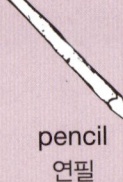

hammer
망치

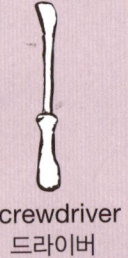

pencil
연필

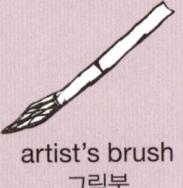

screwdriver
드라이버

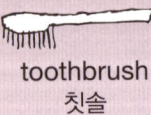

artist's brush
그림붓

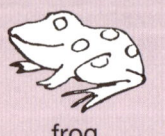

toothbrush
칫솔

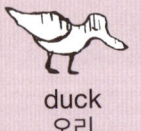

frog
개구리

duck
오리

Illustrated by Valeri Gorbachev

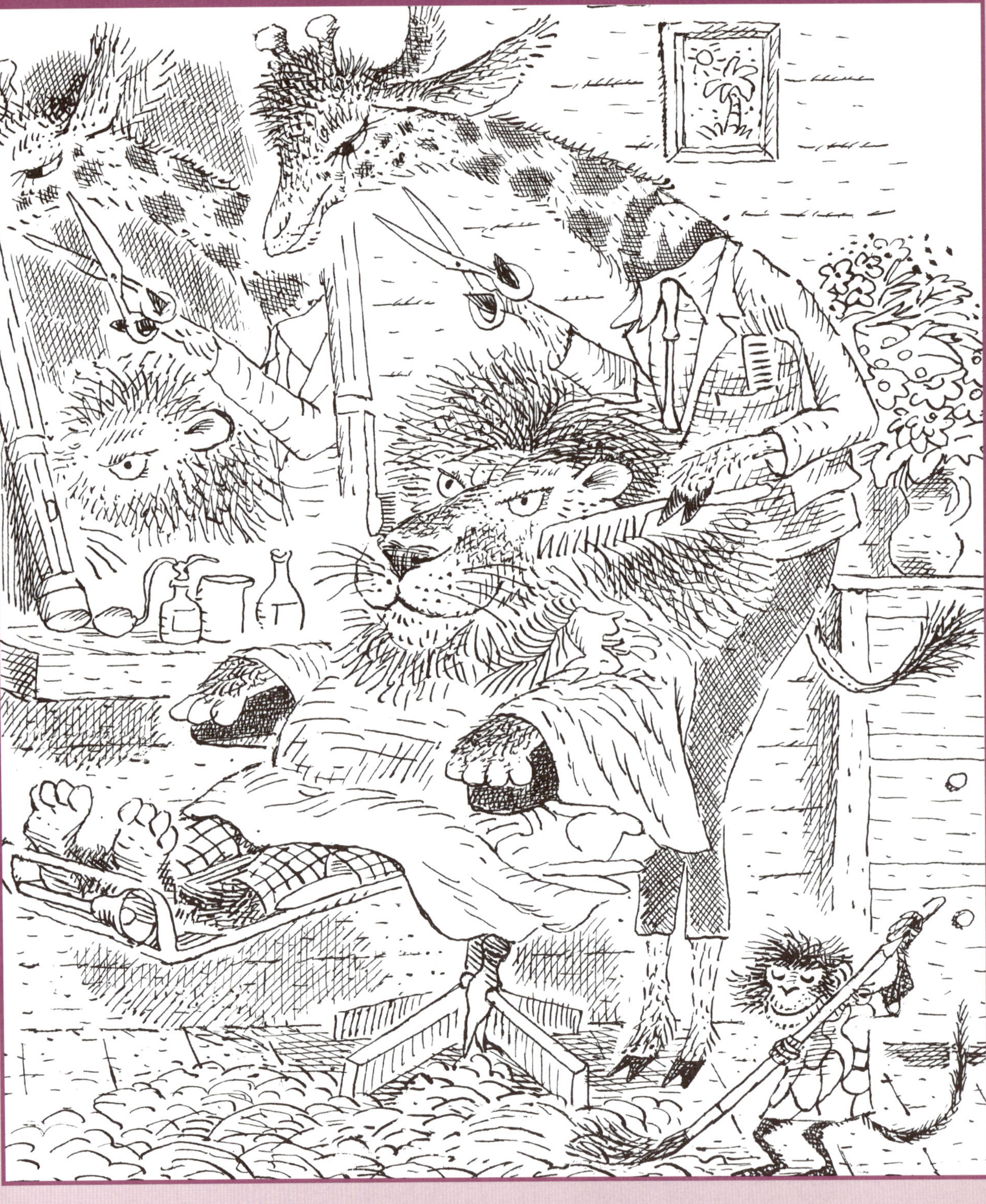

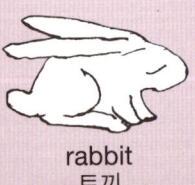

rabbit
토끼

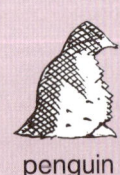

penguin
펭귄

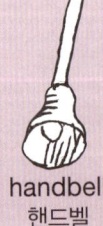

handbell
핸드벨

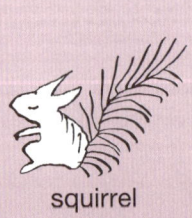

squirrel
다람쥐

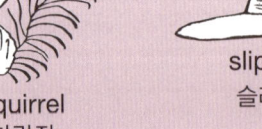

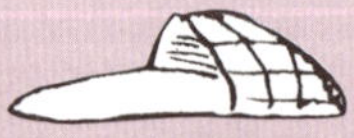

slipper
슬리퍼

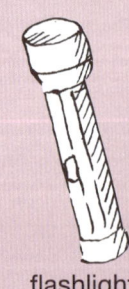

flashlight
손전등

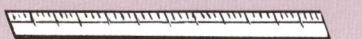
ruler
자

pitcher
물주전자

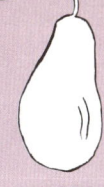
cookie
쿠키

pear
배

ladle
국자

elephant
코끼리

banana
바나나

hat
모자

shoe
신발

The Seamstress 재봉사

hair dryer
헤어드라이어

penguin
펭귄

flashlight
손전등

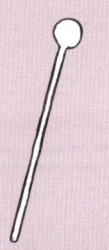
ear of corn
옥수수 낱알

matchstick
성냥개비

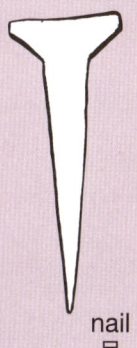
nail
못

Illustrated by Elizabeth Allyn

Highlights **13**

Hippo's Library 하마의 서재

candle
양초

comb
빗

ruler
자

thimble
골무

golf club
골프채

scrub brush
세탁용 솔

drinking straw
빨대

feather
깃털

piece of candy
캔디

heart
하트

toothbrush
칫솔

ice-cream cone
아이스크림 콘

wrench
렌치

hockey stick
하키 스틱

pickle
피클

ladle
국자

Illustrated by Ron Lieser

heart
하트

turtle
거북

cat
고양이

button
단추

mushroom
버섯

bird
새

cupcake
컵케이크

open book
펴놓은 책

sailboat
돛단배

flag
깃발

ice-cream
cone
아이스크림 콘

carrot
당근

pencil
연필

candle
양초

pig
돼지

crescent
moon
초승달

fish
물고기

needle
바늘

Hot Summer Day 무더운 여름날

School Band '쿵짝 쿵짝' 학교 밴드

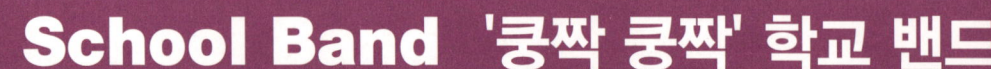

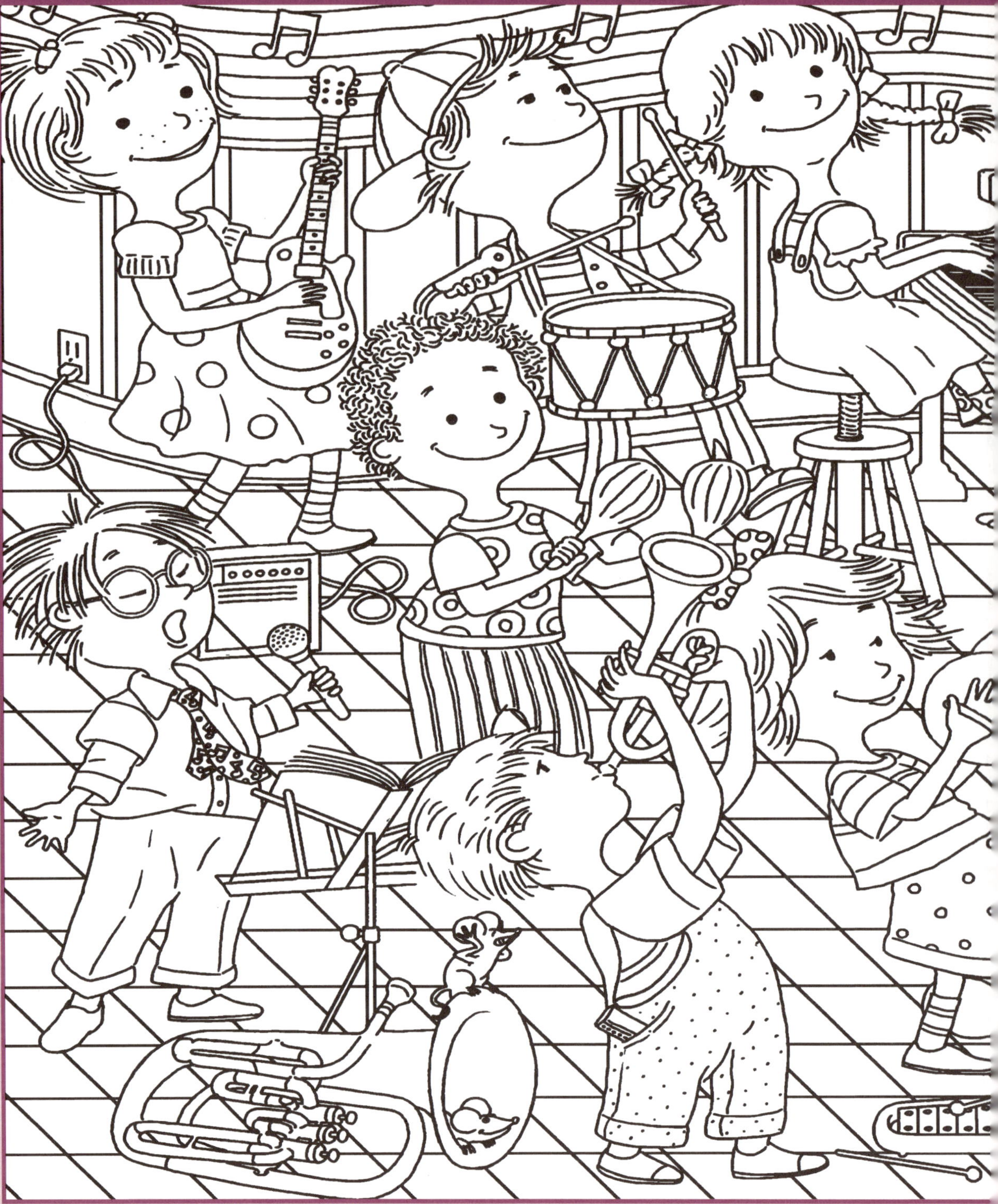

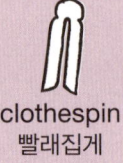

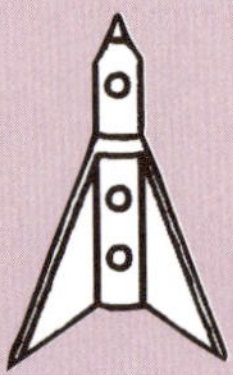
spaceship
우주선

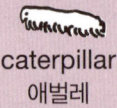

clothespin
빨래집게

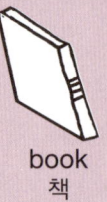

caterpillar
애벌레

book
책

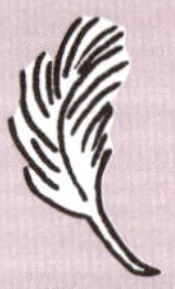

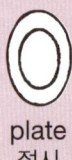

feather
깃털

plate
접시

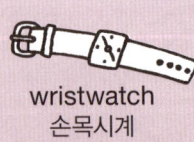

wristwatch
손목시계

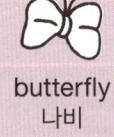

butterfly
나비

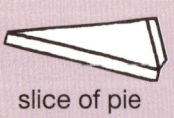

slice of pie
파이 조각

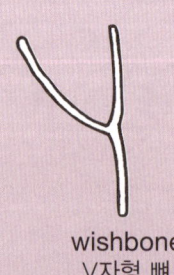

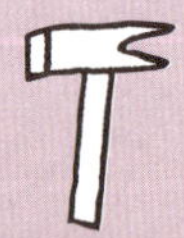
hammer
망치

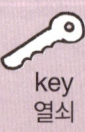

wishbone
V자형 뼈

key
열쇠

pennant
삼각기

cupcake
컵케이크

candle
양초

hat
모자

nail
못

Illustrated by Paul Richer

boomerang
부메랑

sailboat
돛단배

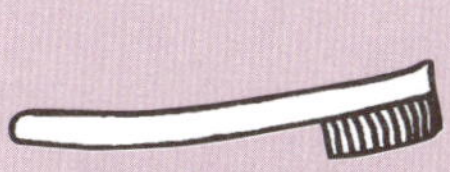

toothbrush
칫솔

teacup
찻잔

crescent moon
초승달

ring
반지

toothbrush
칫솔

sneaker
운동화

light bulb
백열전구

bowling pin
볼링 핀

carrot
당근

spoon
숟가락

snake
뱀

slice of pie
파이 조각

strawberry
딸기

ice-cream bar
막대아이스크림

golf club
골프채

fish
물고기

sailboat
돛단배

bird
새

mallet
나무망치

ice-cream cone
아이스크림 콘

artist's brush
그림붓

candle
양초

Illustrated by Linda Weller

iron
다리미

crayon
크레용

nail
못

magnet
자석

oven mitt
오븐용 장갑

trowel
꽃삽

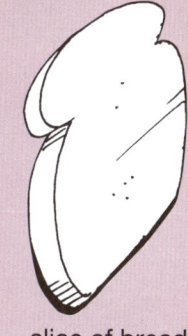

slice of bread
빵 조각

butterfly
나비

fishhook
낚싯바늘

ring
반지

sock
양말

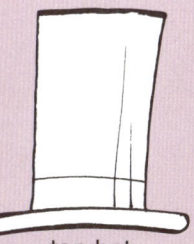

top hat
남성 정장용 모자

lollipop
막대사탕

Soup for Lunch 수프 점심식사

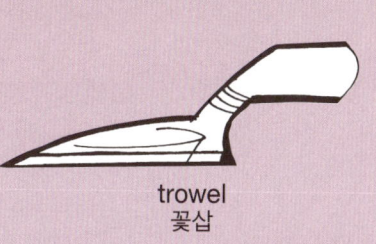

bowling pin
볼링 핀

sock
양말

mug
머그잔

flashlight
손전등

tea bag
차 봉지

pencil
연필

needle
바늘

fishhook
낚싯바늘

Planting Flowers 꽃나무 심기

ring
반지

heart
하트

fork
포크

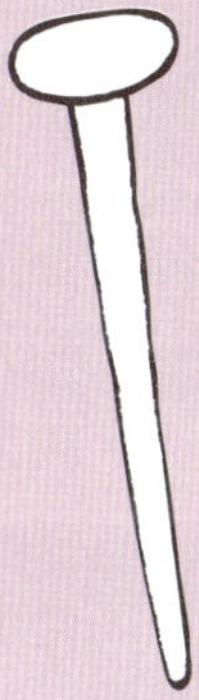

nail
못

spoon
숟가락

flag
깃발

oilcan
기름통

comb
빗

pencil
연필

funnel
깔때기

slice of cake
케이크 조각

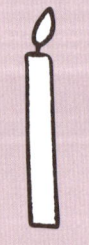
candle
양초

artist's brush
그림붓

snake
뱀

slice of pie
파이 조각

scrub brush
세탁용 솔

cupcake
컵케이크

banana
바나나

feather
깃털

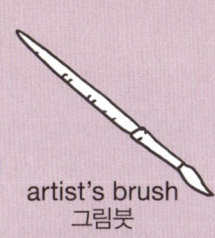

artist's brush
그림붓

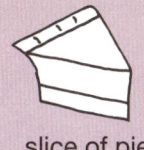

slice of pie
파이 조각

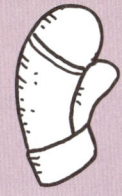

mitten
벙어리장갑

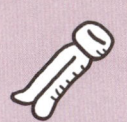

clothespin
빨래집게

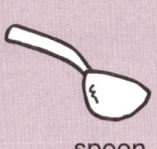

spoon
숟가락

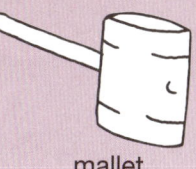

mallet
나무망치

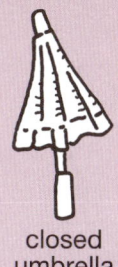

closed umbrella
접은 우산

Barn Dance 시골집에서 열린 춤잔치

Illustrated by Charles Jordan

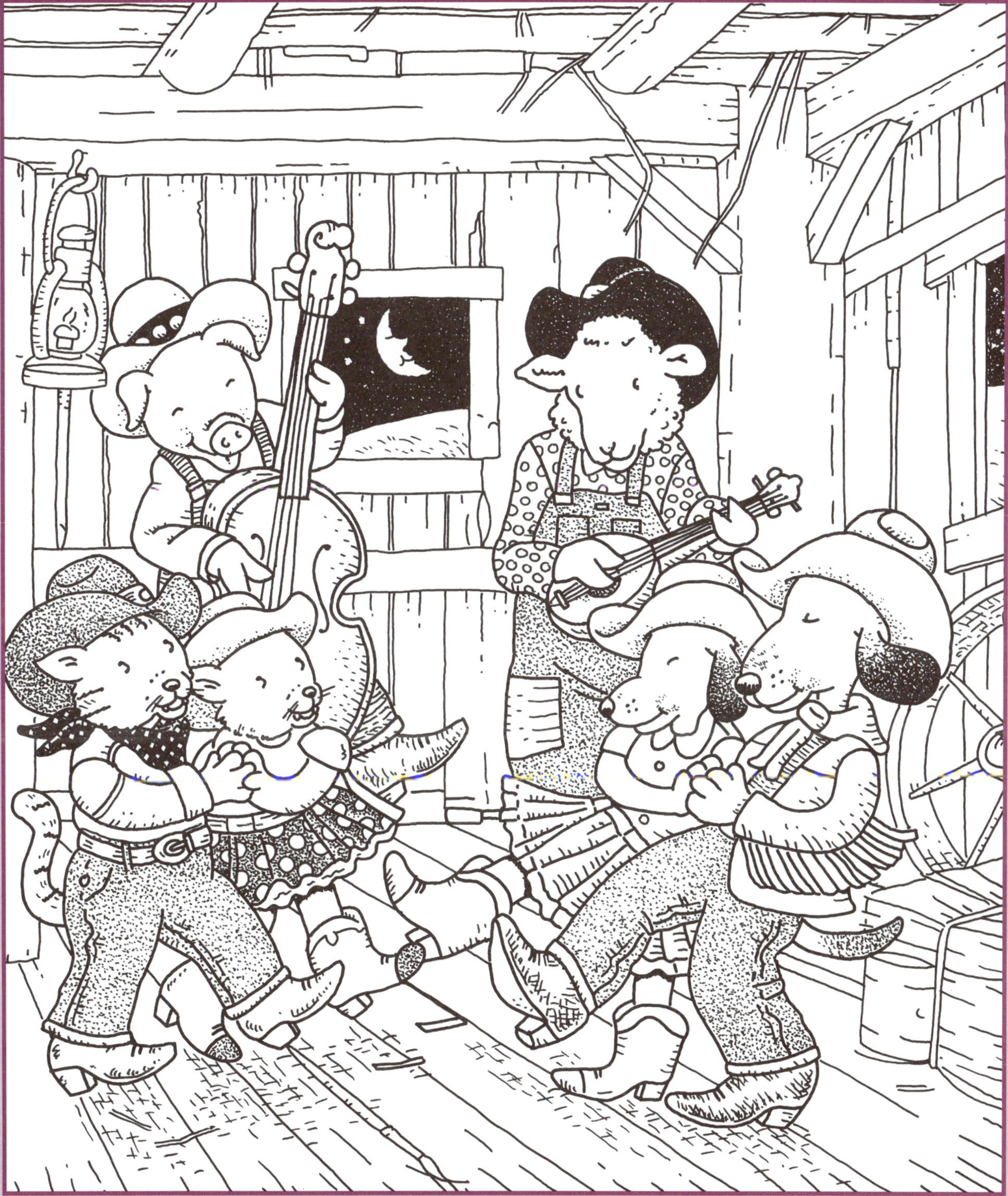

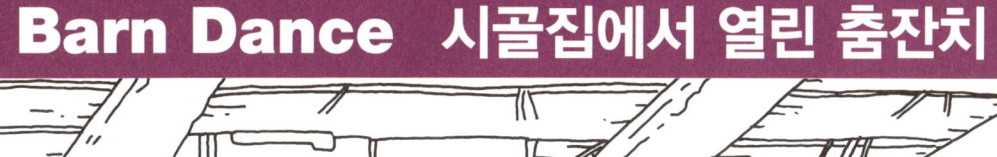

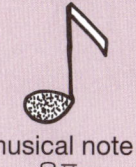

musical note
음표

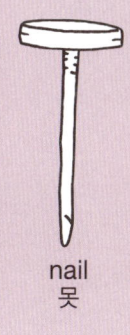

nail
못

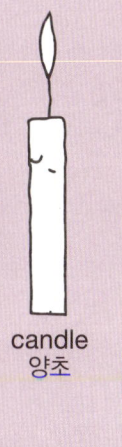

candle
양초

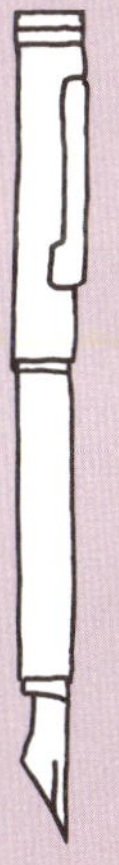

pen
만년필

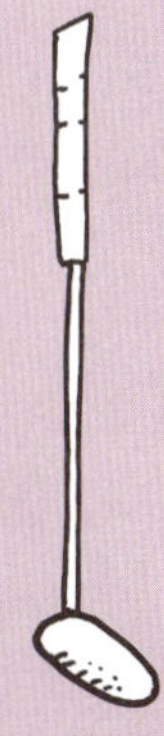

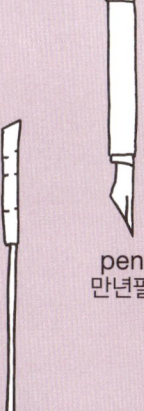

golf club
골프채

Snowy Buffalo 하얗게 눈을 덮어쓴 버펄로

feather
깃털

rabbit
토끼

pencil
연필

frog
개구리

slice of pie
파이 조각

saw
톱

Illustrated by Tim Davis

bat
박쥐

fish
물고기

dog
개

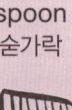
mouse
쥐

spoon
숟가락

comb
빗

dolphin
고래

turtle
거북

Highlights

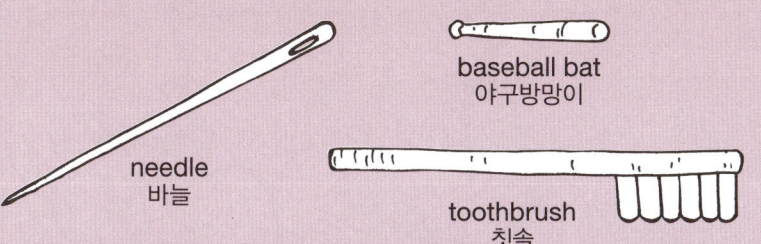

needle
바늘

baseball bat
야구방망이

toothbrush
칫솔

tack
압정

open book
펴놓은 책

goose
거위

Fun at the Playground 놀이터에서 신나게 놀아요

ice-cream cone
아이스크림 콘

heart
하트

cherries
체리

ring
반지

pencil
연필

mallet
나무망치

crown
왕관

pencil
연필

teacup
찻잔

fork
포크

bell
종

safety pin
안전핀

banana
바나나

fish
물고기

goose
거위

turtle
거북

apple
사과

sailboat
돛단배

mitten
벙어리장갑

football
럭비공

bee
벌

heart
하트

candy cane
가락엿

carrot
당근

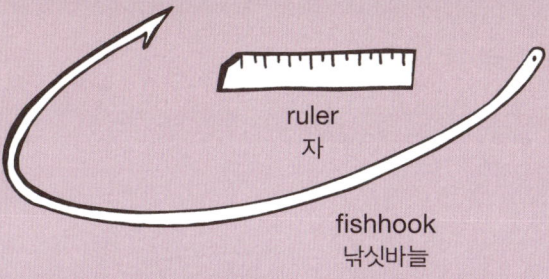
ruler
자

fishhook
낚싯바늘

ice pop
얼음과자

banana
바나나

mug
머그잔

umbrella
우산

Pond Serenade 연못 세레나데

flag
깃발

ladle
국자

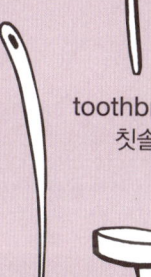
toothbrush
칫솔

needle
바늘

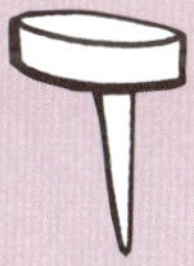

tack
압정

baseball bat
야구방망이

mitten
벙어리장갑

Illustrated by Karen Stormer Brooks

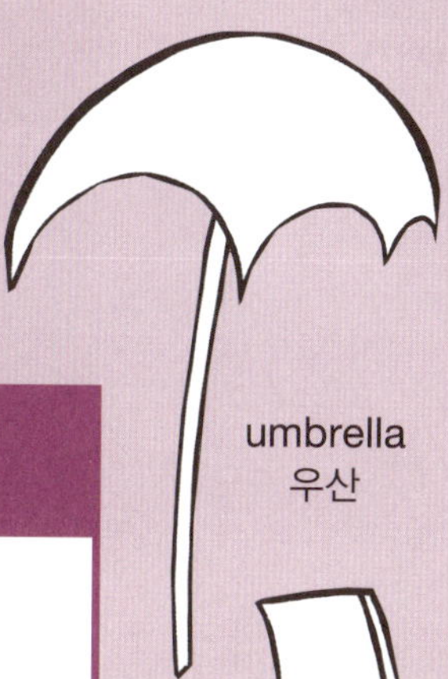

Highlights **27**

tube of
toothpaste
치약튜브

eyeglasses
안경

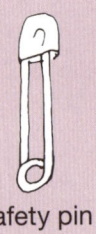

iron
다리미

safety pin
안전핀

baseball
야구공

trowel
꽃삽

key
렌치

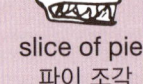

pen
만년필

slice of pie
파이 조각

flower
꽃

crayon
크레용

stepladder
발판사다리

fish
물고기

hammer
망치

paintbrush
페인트붓

Illustrated by Ruth Hovler

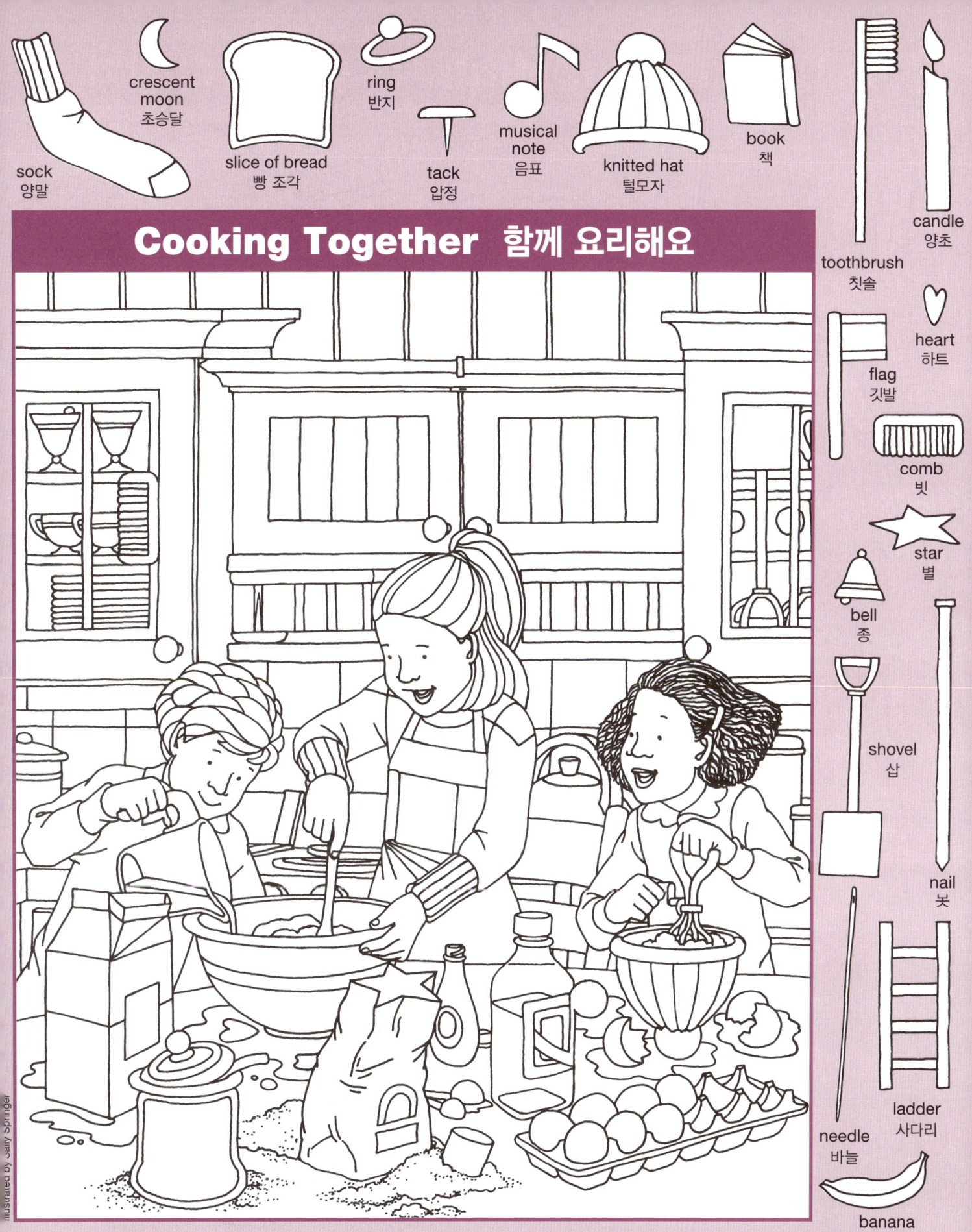

sock 양말
crescent moon 초승달
slice of bread 빵 조각
ring 반지
tack 압정
musical note 음표
knitted hat 털모자
book 책
toothbrush 칫솔
candle 양초
flag 깃발
heart 하트
comb 빗
star 별
bell 종
shovel 삽
nail 못
needle 바늘
ladder 사다리
banana 바나나

Cooking Together 함께 요리해요

spatula
주걱

feather
깃털

hoe
괭이

pencil
연필

dustpan
쓰레받기

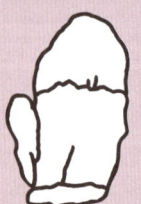
mitten
벙어리장갑

ring
반지

flag
깃발

carrot
당근

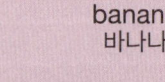
toothbrush
칫솔

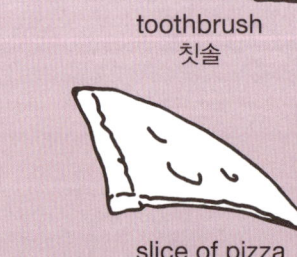
slice of pizza
피자 조각

banana
바나나

slice of cake
케이크 조각

mug
머그잔

Highlights

bicycle pump
자전거 공기주입기

golf club
골프채

book
책

sock
양말

handbag
핸드백

Illustrated by Charles Jordan

sailboat
돛단배

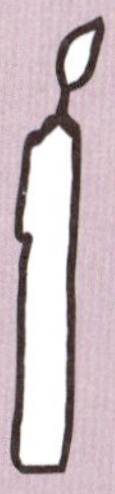

candle
양초

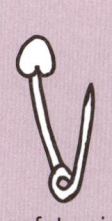

nail
못

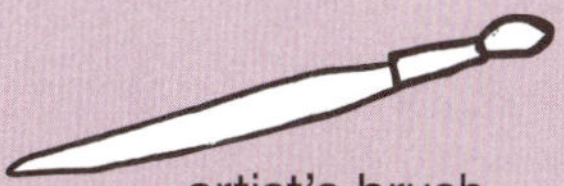

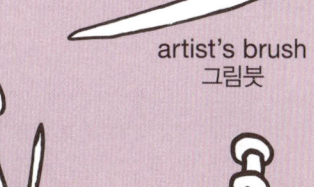

artist's brush
그림붓

safety pin
안전핀

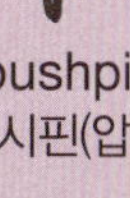

pushpin
푸시핀(압정)

tube of
toothpaste
치약튜브

slice of pie
파이 조각

Trip to Australia 동물들의 오스트레일리아 여행

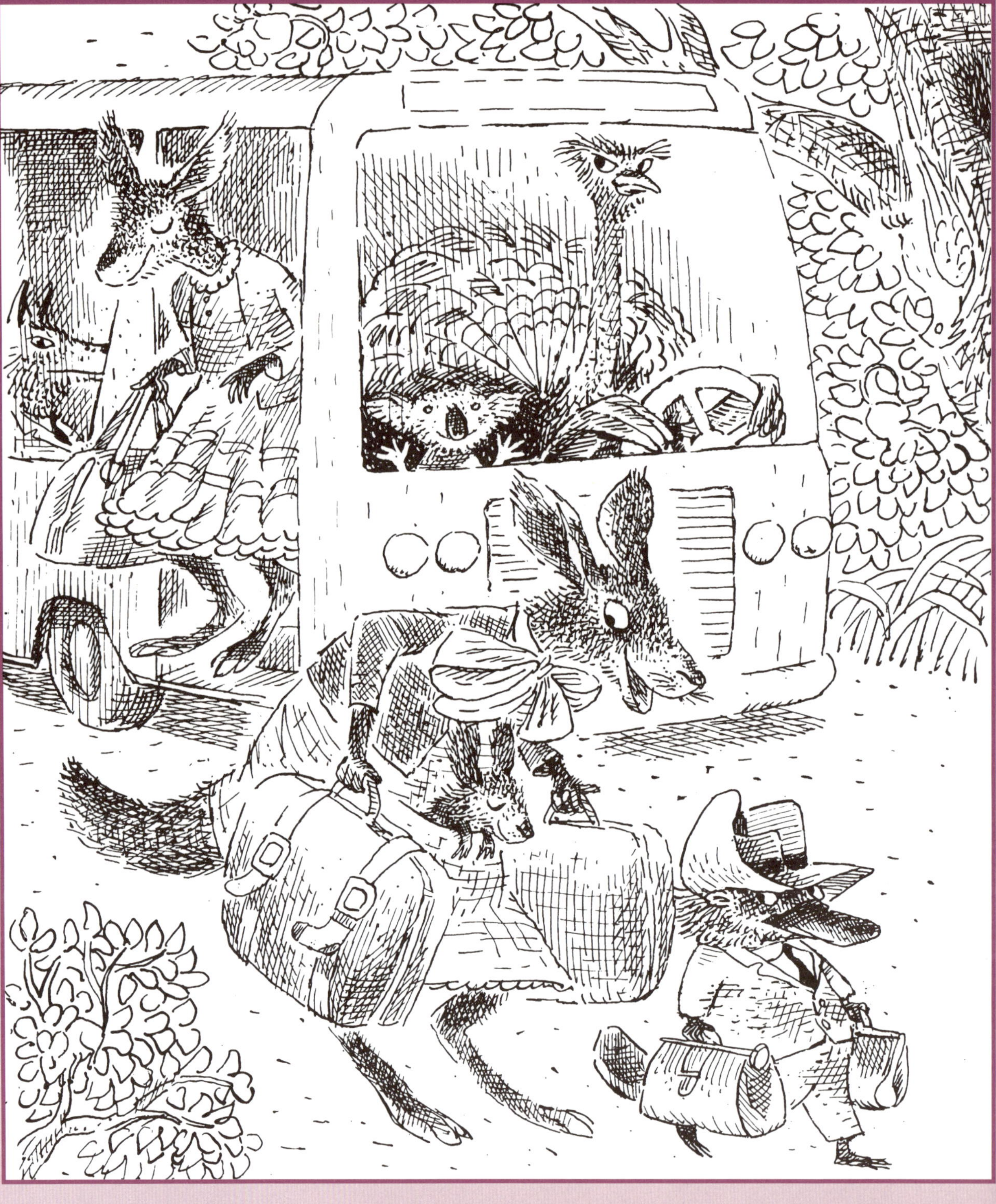

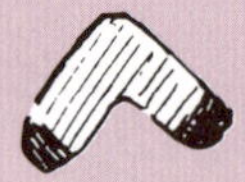

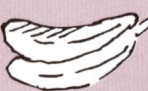

boomerang
부메랑

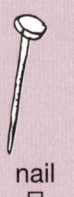

2 bananas
바나나 두 개

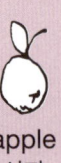

nail
못

apple
사과

sock
양말

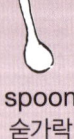

spoon
숟가락

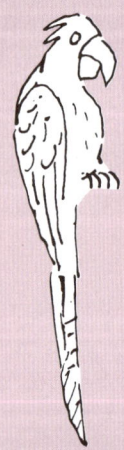

parrot
앵무새

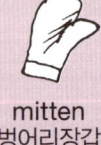

mitten
벙어리장갑

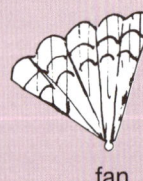

fan
부채

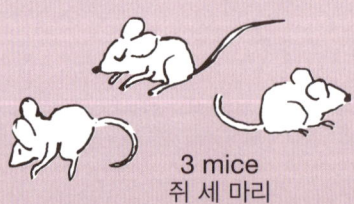

3 mice
쥐 세 마리

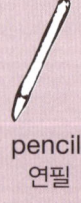

pencil
연필

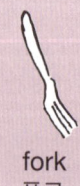

fork
포크

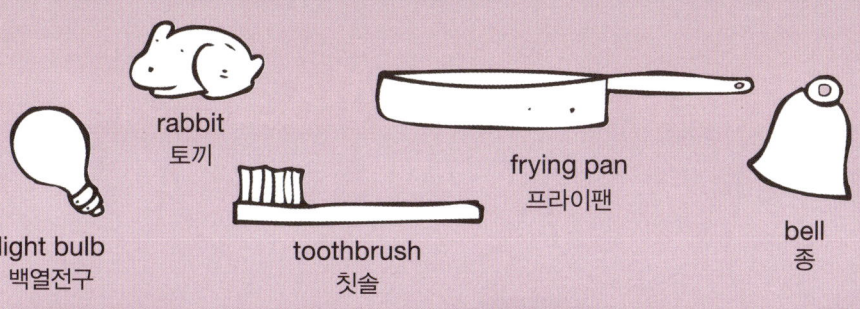

light bulb
백열전구

rabbit
토끼

toothbrush
칫솔

frying pan
프라이팬

bell
종

pencil
연필

broccoli
브로콜리

For Me? 나한테 주는 거야?

paper clip
클립

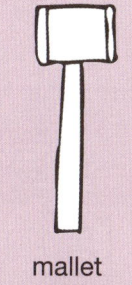

mallet
나무망치

artist's
brush
그림붓

teacup
찻잔

safety pin
안전핀

Illustrated by Mary Sullivan

Ice-Cream Stand 맛있는 아이스크림 가게

book
책

party horn
파티 나팔

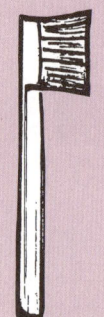
toothbrush
칫솔

snail
달팽이

mug
머그잔

Illustrated by Arieh Zeldich

fishhook
낚싯바늘

ring
반지

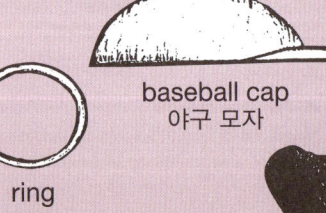
baseball cap
야구 모자

heart
하트

whale
고래

seashell
조개껍질

ladle
국자

34 **Highlights**

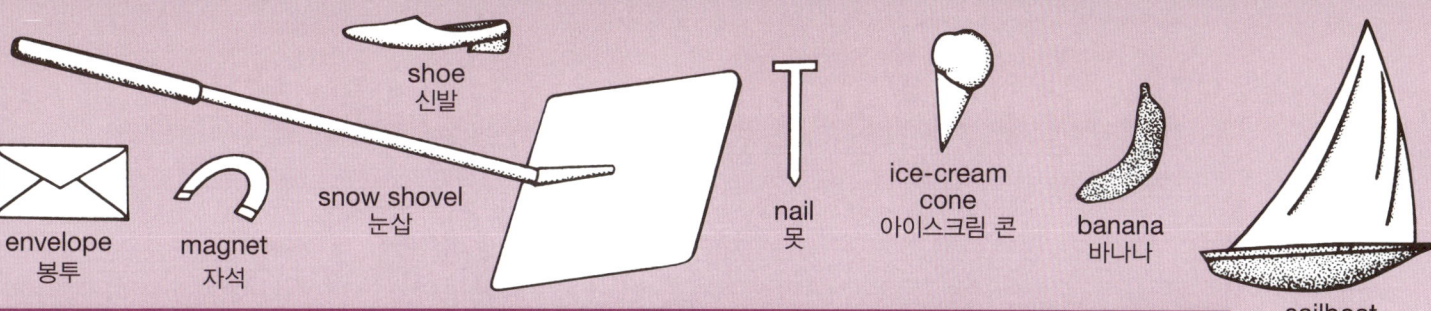

envelope
봉투

magnet
자석

shoe
신발

snow shovel
눈삽

nail
못

ice-cream
cone
아이스크림 콘

banana
바나나

sailboat
돛단배

Practicing the Duet 시끄러운 이중주 연습

crescent
moon
초승달

candle
양초

lemon
레몬

ice-cream bar
막대아이스크림

party hat
파티 모자

slice of bread
빵 조각

otter
수달

goose
거위

high-heeled
shoe
굽 높은 신발

arrow
화살표

oar
노

sailboat
돛단배

seashell
조개껍질

sheep
양

camel
낙타

eyeglasses
안경

2 birds
새 두 마리

ballerina
발레리나

anteater
개미핥기

shark
상어

artist's
brush
그림붓

lizard
도마뱀

2 fish
물고기 두 마리

cat
고양이

umbrella
우산

car
자동차

chicken
닭

sailboat
돛단배

pen
만년필

fork
포크

comb
빗

heart
하트

sock
양말

Dog Days 너무 더운 날

crescent moon
초승달

needle
바늘

spoon
숟가락

apple core
사과 속

light bulb
백열전구

mop
대걸레

Skating Together 모두 함께 스케이트 타요

mitten
벙어리장갑

sock
양말

carrot
당근

flag
깃발

comb
빗

pennant
삼각기

domino
도미노 패

pie
파이

lollipop
막대사탕

muffin
머핀

crown
왕관

heart
하트

ice-cream
cone
아이스크림 콘

slice of pie
파이 조각

nail
못

leaf
나뭇잎

bowl
그릇

needle
바늘

envelope
봉투

slice of bread
빵 조각

Highlights

bugle
나팔

bell
종

sailboat
돛단배

hat
모자

carrot
당근

dolphin
고래

pennant
삼각기

toothbrush
칫솔

tack
압정

paintbrush
페인트붓

mushroom
버섯

slice of pie
파이 조각

mug
머그잔

heart
하트

funnel
깔때기

crescent
moon
초승달

candle
양초

ring
반지

needle
바늘

oar
노

Trail Ride 말 타고 오솔길 산책하기

Illustrated by Linda Weller

▼2~3페이지

▼4페이지

▼5페이지

▼6페이지

▼7페이지

▼8페이지

▼9페이지

레이크우드
지역주민들의
정원

▼10페이지

▼11페이지

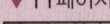

▼12페이지

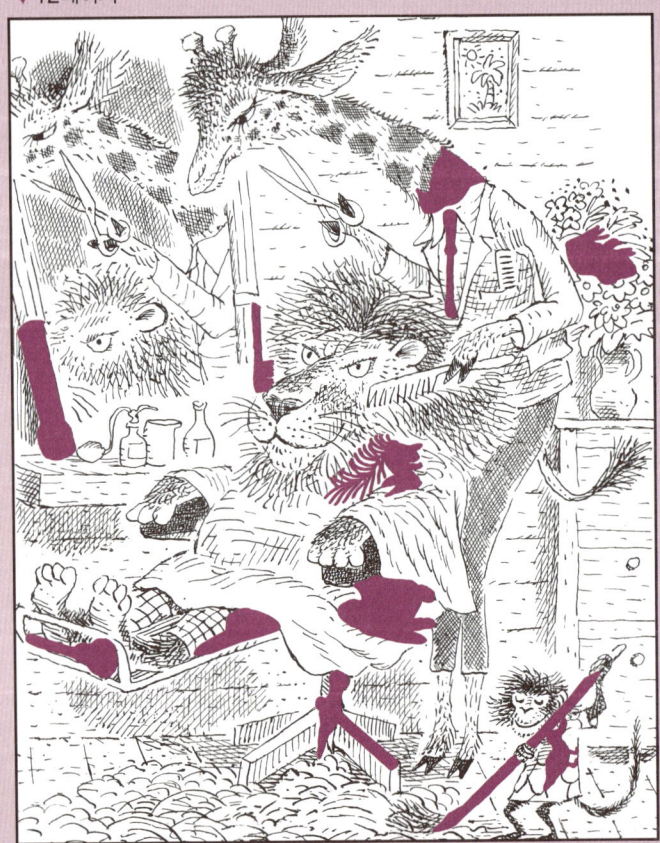

▼13페이지

▼14페이지

▼15페이지

▼16~17페이지

정답

▼18페이지

▼19페이지

▼20페이지

▼21페이지

▼22페이지

▼23페이지

▼24페이지

▼25페이지

정답

▼26페이지

▼27페이지

▼28페이지

▼29페이지

▼30~31페이지

▼32페이지

▼33페이지

정답

▼34페이지

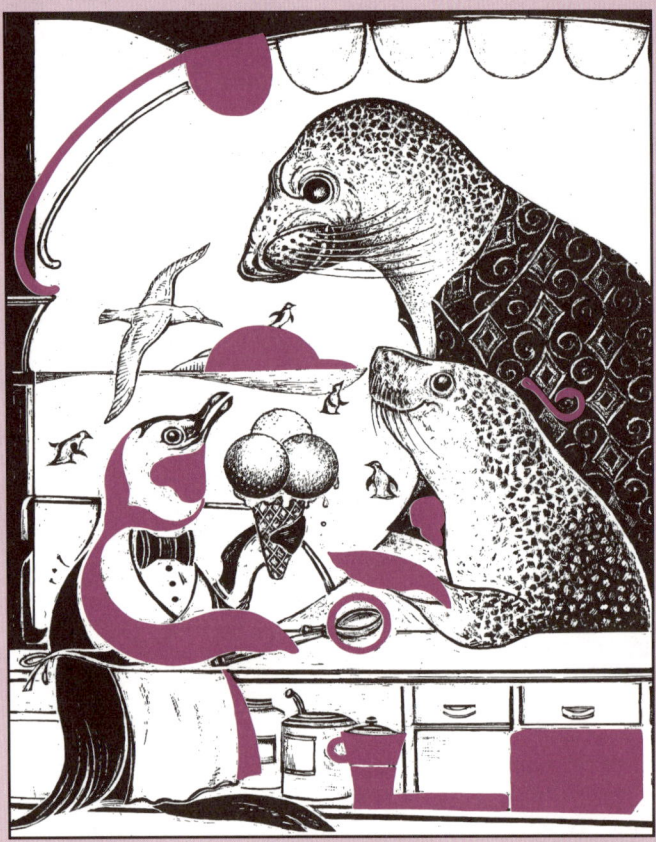

▼35페이지

▼36페이지

▼37페이지